Democracy on the Shop Floor?

An American Look at Employee Influence in Scandinavia Today

EDITED BY

ERIC S. EINHORN AND JOHN LOGUE

Picture credits:

Pp. 14, 38, Historiska Museet, Gothenburg; p. 15,
Jonny Johansson and Götaverken Arendal AB; pp. 24, 67,
Arbejderbevægelsens Bibliotek og Arkiv, Copenhagen;
p. 38, SKF; p. 60, Swedish Information Service, New
York.

Cover photos:

First of May demonstration, Trondheim, Norway, 1910;
Arbeiderbevegelsens Arkiv og Bibliotek, Oslo. Consul-
tation at Oxelösunds Järnverk; Development Council for
Collaboration Questions, Stockholm.

ISBN 0-933522-11-8

Printed and distributed by
Kent Popular Press
P.O. Box 715
Kent, Ohio 44240

HD
8540
D4

CONTENTS

Preface   5

Democracy on the Shop Floor   9

Comparative Industrial Relations   25

A Different Industrial Reality: Observations
  in Swedish Plants   30

What Can Americans Learn from Scandinavians?
  A Roundtable Discussion   56

Final Comment   79

PREFACE

Industrial relations is in the throes of transformation. The causes are varied. The accelerating changes in production technology -- increasing computerization, growing use of industrial robots, and the like -- are altering the nature of work in offices and factories. Increasing employee expectations and education levels have undermined traditional managerial practices. The rise of the multinational corporation and the creation of a global market have shifted the balance of power between union and management.

The impact of these changes on industrial relations has become increasingly clear in Europe in the last decade. A wave of experimentation brought job redesign, expanded bargaining power for unions, employee board representation, and, occasionally, the creation of employee-run companies. The economic crisis of the late 1970s in the United States has led to innovation on this side of the Atlantic as well, ranging from union access to company books and union representation on corporate boards to employee take-overs of failing firms, though more as a product of desperation than as a coherent strategy for extending democracy into working life.

Democratization of work has gone further in Scandinavia than elsewhere in Europe. Job redesign projects, pushed by management and unions alike, have produced real changes in work, including the abolition of the assembly line in some auto plants. Co-determination arrangements, including works councils and the Swedish Employee Participation Act that requires employers to initiate negotiations on all important decisions, have given employees and their organizations new sources of information and influence. Health and safety legislation has brought major changes on the shop floor, especially with the institution of a system of safety stewards to enforce the law. Employee representatives on corporate boards have introduced a pluralism of views into corporate deliberations. And the managerial response -- and this never fails to shock Americans -- is basically positive.

Individually, these changes are significant; as a group, their implications are far-reaching.

This booklet developed out of a workshop designed to examine these "new directions in industrial relations." The workshop was organized under the auspices of the Council for European Studies and the Scandinavian Seminar College.* It was not an academic meeting in which specialist talked to specialist, but cut across all lines of work, specialization, and training. It brought together American and Scandinavian trade unionists from the shop floor as well as national offices, university teachers and researchers, government officials, and others with diverse experience in cooperatives, political organizations, and the like for a week's conference in Holte, just north of Copenhagen. The workshop continued for a group of the American participants with visits to a series of Swedish plants to see how the various Swedish reforms worked in practice.

---

*"New Directions in Industrial Relations: An American-Scandinavian Workshop" was sponsored by the Council for European Studies, Kent State University's Department of Political Science, Scandinavian Seminar College, and the University of Massachusetts (Amherst). It was made possible by the financial support of the American-Scandinavian Foundation, the Council for European Studies, the Danish Metal Workers Federation, the German Marshall Fund of the United States, Linköping University, the Nordic Cultural Foundation, Scandinavian Seminar College, the Swedish Institute, and the Swedish Information Service. The study trip was arranged with the help of the Swedish Metal Workers Federation. We appreciate the support of these groups and the hospitality of the Metal Workers locals at SKF, Götaverken, Saab-Trollhätten, and Volvo-Skövde, which made the study visits very pleasant.

This report focuses on those study visits. Our concerns were those of the Holte conference: employee influence on managerial decisions, especially on the introduction of new technology and on health and safety; job redesign; problems of plant closings; and the relation of the Scandinavian reforms to the political and trade union context. The unsigned sections of the report were written by Eric Einhorn and John Logue. Einhorn bears principal responsibility for "A Different Industrial Reality"; Logue, for "Democracy on the Shop Floor?" Bob Cooney's "Dealing with Technological Change," written originally for the American trade union press, appears by courtesy of Press Associates Inc. The discussion of how to go about comparing American and Scandinavian labor relations was written by Howard Gospel, an English observer of both the American and Scandinavian labor scenes, who brings the genuinely comparative perspective of the outsider to bear on both. The views expressed are, of course, those of the authors, and are not the responsibility of the organizations that sponsored the workshop. Similarly, trade union and university affiliations are provided for roundtable discussants for purpose of identification only; the views expressed there are those of the individuals.

The rapid transformation of contemporary economic and technological conditions demands increased communication between practitioners and researchers in industrial relations both within national systems and between them. In both conference presentations and field visits the workshop participants saw indisputable evidence of the internationalization of production, management, and planning. Many of the reforms in industrial relations are vulnerable to international trade, investment and management. Counterbalancing, at least in part, these constraints on national labor relations is the opportunity to learn from the experience of others. Despite the rhetoric of trade union internationalism, too many American unions have been consistently provincial in attitudes and information. But the problems we face are common to all Western industrial societies, and the multinationals have increased our interdependence. We need to know how others have tackled the problems. And given the decentralization of collective bargaining in many American industries, it is not sufficient that union headquarters are well informed about comparative labor relations. That knowledge belongs much closer to the shop floor.

This report seeks to make some of what the workshop participants heard and saw, especially in Swedish plants, available to a wider public. We do not mean to suggest that the elements of Scandinavian industrial relations can be transplanted directly to other systems. But there is much in the Scandinavian innovations in industrial relations worthy of thoughtful consideration.

December 1981   Eric Einhorn & John Logue

Democracy on the Shop Floor?

Imagine yourself on a production line. The guard on your machine has broken off. You point it out to your foreman. He tells you to be careful; they'll fix it during routine maintenance the day after tomorrow. Your union safety representative agrees that "that thing can take your hand off," as he puts it to the foreman. "He can watch out; hell, we're running a production line, not a nursery," replies the foreman. What happens? The safety steward shuts the line down, and the law says he has a right to. The law also says you, and the other people on the line, get paid until the company fixes the safety guard.

You're a 58 year old machinist, had a mild heart attack three months ago, and have been back at work for three weeks. Your boss calls you in and says, "Joe, I'm real sorry to say this. I know you've worked here for 11 years, but we're going to have to let you go. You're nowhere close to meeting production norms, and everybody here has to do his share." You reply, "Mr. Svensson, you can't fire me; I've got two kids still at home, & my wife's sick. You have to find work I can do." What happens? The law says you're right: he can't.

You're a twenty-three year old woman in a auto assembly plant. You're pregnant, and you want to take your seven months of paid maternity leave so that you have as much time with the baby as possible after it's born. But the doctor says less lifting, you're having trouble keeping the pace, and you're only starting your fifth month. What do you do? Start your maternity leave now and end up with only ten weeks at home with the baby? No! You ask to be transferred to the rehabilitation group that assembles auto doors at a

9

*much slower pace -- it's possible to have different
rates of speed in the same assembly department, because
the assembly line has been abolished, and team assembly
is much more flexible.*

*You're the chairman of the local union at a roller
bearing plant. Your predecessor spent most of his time
negotiating wages and dealing with grievances; that was
his job. That's only half of your job. The other half
is bargaining with management about investment decisions, production plans and appointment of managerial
personnel. Management can ultimately impose its decisions, but the plant manager has appointed no one to a
middle managerial position in the last 10 years who did
not have union approval.*

*You're the plant manager, confronted for the last
5 years with the curious system of informing the union
and negotiating matters you used to decide by yourself.
A foreign visitor asks you how the system really works.
You pause a moment to consider, for while you deal with
specific questions within this system every day, you
are far too busy to spend much time considering such
theoretical questions. After all, you've got to run
a stamping plant. You light your pipe and reply:
  Well, I guess we end up with better solutions.
  No, I'd go farther. We come up with more effective, more correct decisions. We have to ex-
  plain what we want to do. If we can't defend
  it, we shouldn't do it.*

This cast of characters is not drawn from utopian
fiction. Nor is it "after the revolution." This
is everyday working life in Sweden. Each of these
five cases is a real person. Twelve or fourteen
years ago they -- or people in their shoes -- were in
the same situation as American workers. If you were
on the line, you tried to be real careful until the
company got round to fixing that guard, and hoped it
was next week, not next month. The role of the union
was to get maximum wages from the employer and social
benefits from government so that members had the

wherewithal to enjoy their leisure time. The manager
was expected to make his decisions in splendid soli-
tude. Employees could accept those decisions or
protest them, but they could not negotiate them.

But the systematic reforms of the last decade have
changed life on the job in Sweden in some very fundamental ways:

● Job redesign experiments -- which have become
so numerous and well established that they can hardly
be classified as experimental today -- have begun to
reverse the fragmentation of the work process that
has been the essence of "scientific management"
throughout this century.

● Increased individual rights -- to maternity and
paternity leave, to language instruction for foreign
workers on company time, to leave of absence for
study, and, above all else, to job security -- have
strengthened the position of the individual employee
vis-à-vis his employer.

● Increased collective rights for employees to
board representation -- to full information about the
company, to negotiate all questions of importance
including investment decisions, layoffs, production
plans, and managerial appointments -- have given
employees as a group substantial influence on management.

● And health and safety legislation has transferred substantial amounts of power from management
to safety stewards in all matters concerning health
and safety.

It is an impressive catalog of reforms for any
decade, especially the stagnant Seventies.

THE CONTEXT MAKES A LOT OF DIFFERENCE

All Americans are democrats in theory. It is just
our practice that is schizophrenic. Democracy stops
at the office door and the factory gate. Outside,
you are a citizen. You speak your mind, vote as you
see fit, run for office. Inside, you are a subject
of managerial absolutism. Free speech is insubordi-

nation, and the only way to vote is with your feet, which is an expensive sort of ballot. The idea of running for your boss's job seems ludicrous. But is it?

A quiet revolution throughout Western Europe is extending democracy into working life. A gradual expansion of the scope of collective bargaining, increasing employee influence on the shop floor and in the board room, and collective stock purchases have all contributed to opening up the workplace. For a variety of reasons the Scandinavians, particularly the Swedes, have taken these reforms further than elsewhere.

A look at what has happened in Sweden gives some sense of the potential of industrial democracy. It also gives a sense of the contradictory forces involved. Employees and employers share a common interest in overhauling the structure of authority at work. But their motivations are as divergent as the problems they face. High rates of absenteeism and employee turnover plague employers. Well-educated manual workers express extreme discontent with jobs their parents were happy to hold. Unions find that taxes take most of their members' wage increases.

The solutions chosen to these individual problems are combined in the current confused, composite definition of industrial and economic democracy: redesigning jobs to fit workers rather than vice versa; job security; job safety; expanding the scope of collective bargaining to encompass organizing work, investment policy, and other managerial prerogatives; increasing worker influence on the shop floor; putting employee representatives on company boards; and redistributing stock ownership. The cumulative impact of these changes promises to be a redistribution of authority on the job as revolutionary as the centralization that resulted from the imposition of the factory system in the last century. The effects of democratization are only beginning to be felt, but the balance of power on the job between capital and labor is already shifting in some fundamental ways.

The fact that the Swedes in particular and the Scandinavians in general have gone farther to extend democracy into working life than others is a product of the political context and the structure of labor relations there. Five key contextual factors distinguish the Swedish situation from that in the United States.

First, much of the appeal for workers of increasing influence on the job in Sweden stems from the combination of high wages, excellent social benefits, and high taxes. This has affected the popular ranking of reforms. The most basic material needs have been satisfied. Furthermore, social programs provide security against a catastrophic decline in standard of living through illness, old age, unemployment, or disability, and reduce the need for savings. Special benefits and transfer payments raise the real income of low wage workers with large families to something not too far below the national average. Moreover, it is less important to push wages up today than it was twenty years ago simply because the high taxes necessary to support the social welfare system have dramatically reduced the marginal utility of wage increases: the high marginal tax rates means that at least half of any wage increase lands in government coffers. Priority has gradually shifted away from increasing money income to increasing non-money income, such as satisfaction on the job. In fact, recent Swedish studies indicate that self-determination on the job increases job satisfaction far more than higher money wages do.

Second, Sweden is highly unionized. About three-quarters of the Swedish labor force is covered by collective bargaining, as contrasted to roughly one-quarter in the U. S. Besides providing the Swedish Social Democrats with the political muscle that kept them in power from 1932 to 1976, the high degree of organization has kept wages apace with inflation for almost all workers; in the United States, the unorganized majority has borne the brunt of the fight against inflation with the marked erosion of its real income.

The hull of a ship under construction at Eriksbergs Mekaniska Verkstad, around the turn of the century. Eriksberg, one of Gothenburg's four major yards, fell victim to the contraction of the shipbuilding industry. It was closed in 1978.

The Arendal yard has been converted to construction of offshore drilling platforms.

The high organization percent in Sweden bears with it potential for high wage inflation that would price the Swedes out of the world market, were it not for wage restraint exercised through centralized national bargaining. Swedish contracts are negotiated centrally at the national level between the national labor federation (Landsorganisationen i Sverige - LO) and employers' confederation (Svenska Arbetsgivare - föreningen - SAF). Central negotiations have permitted the pursuit of the "solidaristic wage policy" which increases the income of the most poorly paid relative to the well paid, artificially raising wages in low wage industries (thereby, incidentally, tending to force them out of existence) and restraining them in high wage industries. This is particularly important in the capital intensive Swedish export industries where a high rate of investment (and therefore profitability) is necessary to maintain exports. Needless to say, over time this policy has generated considerable opposition -- and some wildcat strikes -- among those who see that it reduces their own money income. Industrial democracy offers an excellent means to provide them with non-monetary benefits.

Third, the Social Democratic-trade union alliance which ran Sweden from 1932 to 1976 put a high priority on keeping unemployment in check. The non-socialist government since 1976 has continued the policy. In recent years, Swedes have held unemployment below 2% through a variety of counter-cyclical policies. There are clearly some limits on how long such policies can keep extended world recessions from the Swedish door, but it is clear that the low level of unemployment has provided a basis for an offensive strategy by Swedish unions. Moreover, the consequence of full employment is that it is easy for employees to change jobs. You can choose where you want to work. The consequence of the excellent system of sick pay - 90% of pay up to a ceiling at roughly a skilled industrial worker's pay -- is that you can choose when you want to work. This combination obviously produces a substantial expansion in individual freedom. It has also increased rates of turnover and absenteeism in monotonous, exhausting, and dirty jobs to the point that job redesign and increasing worker satisfaction become vital for any manager who wants to maintain a stable, competent labor force.

Fourth, Sweden has to export to survive. This not only means that when Swedish wage increases outpace those elsewhere, the Swedes price themselves out of the international market, it also means that maintaining market position requires that the rate of investment in Sweden match or exceed that of Sweden's competitors. But the country's high level of economic security tends to produce a fall in the rate of individual savings. Rather than increase savings through tax breaks for the wealthy, the Swedes have turned to collective forms of savings, most notably the supplemental pension trust funds, and the proposed Wage Earner Funds which will vest ownership of a substantial part of new capital in employees collectively.

Last, but certainly not least, industrial and economic democracy fill an important political role for the labor movement. In the late 1960s, sympathetic foreign observers judged the Swedish labor movement to have every reason for satisfaction. The welfare state that it had constructed had become the model for those who shared its aims elsewhere, an object of emulation and envy. Its record in managing the economy was unparalleled. But instead of self-congratulations, Swedish Social Democrats embarked on a bout of self-criticism that focused on the persistence of inequality amid Social Democratic achievement. The report of the party-trade union "equality commission," headed by Alva Myrdal, pictured a Sweden that had achieved substantial affluence but still fell far short of the egalitarian goals of the labor movement. The report, which appeared in 1969 as the student rebellion reached Swedish shores and wildcat strikes shut down the Gothenburg docks and the iron mines of Norrbotten, drove its political point home:

Certainly our living conditions have been improved and made more equal since the beginning of the century, but our expectations have also

17

risen. Relative to the greater opportunities
created by technological and economic progress, the task of developing a society ...
that respects and encourages the development
of the individual, has also grown ... National
and municipal 'politics' are not enough. The
demand for equality has to be raised everywhere.

The place where inequality remained most thoroughly
entrenched in everyday life was on the job.

Swedish labor is not revolutionary. Party and
unions alike are stalwartly reformist, and proud of
it. Yet there is a deep current of egalitarianism
in the Swedish labor movement that legitimates
ideologically the push for industrial democracy, and
the labor movement has so thoroughly dominated
Swedish politics that there are few in the political
center who would argue against the principle of
greater democracy at work. (In fact, both the
Liberal Party and the agrarian Center Party endorsed
the idea in the early 1970s.) That ideological
hegemony is missing in the United States. Perhaps
alone in the West, we continue to regard managerial
absolutism as ideologically desirable.

THE REFORMS ENUMERATED

The reforms of the 1970s were designed to strengthen
the position of employees individually and collectively. Even the exception to that rule -- managerial
initiatives in redesigning jobs ("humanization of
worklife" in American terminology) -- had some of
those same results not only because of the strength
of the unions but also because Swedish management
recognized that the root cause of the absenteeism and
turnover which were cutting quality and raising costs
was that this generation of blue and white collar
workers is better educated than the last, that its
expectations are higher, and that it believes that
work should not just be steady and well paid but
reasonably interesting as well. Productivity could

not be increased by cosmetic changes by changing the color scheme or getting rid of the reserved parking space for the boss. The bottom line was that it required increasing the individual's ability to control his own work.

The major reforms of the decade can be sketched quickly.

(1) Job redesign: While management's experiments in redesigning jobs have been numerous – the employers' federation has published a summary of some 500 – the most notable departure has been the abolition of the assembly line where it originated, in the auto industry. Both Saab and Volvo have replaced assembly lines with team assembly in some plants. At Saab's Södertalje plant south of Stockholm, engine assembly has been taken over by teams of three who set their own pace; each member has learned to assemble an engine individually. At Volvo's newest assembly plant at Kalmar in southern Sweden, this principle has been extended to all aspects of assembly. While this has not made mass production an outlet for individual creativity, it has reduced the deadening repetition of the assembly line.

Some of the most innovative reforms have broken the cardinal rule of Taylorism that physical and mental work should be separate. At Saab's Trollhättan plant where team assembly has replaced the line in the body assembly department, the teams not only manage their own affairs (eliminating some foremen) and do most repairs on their machinery but also do quality control, train new employees, and do their own budgeting.

(2) Job security: Like their American counterparts, Swedish companies had a strong tendency to dump older workers in favor of younger ones. It was profitable, and taxpayers picked up the tab by paying social welfare benefits to the older workers. Then, in 1974, job security was mandated in Sweden. Although the job security act has made it more difficult for young people to find work, it has protected older workers and it has stimulated employers to distribute work loads more evenly.

(3) Safety: With the "Work Environment Acts" that went into effect in 1974 and 1978, the initiative on health and safety has passed from employers and understaffed government agencies to those most immediately concerned - employees. Workers' representatives, called "safety stewards," are entitled to shut down production that poses immediate danger and to initiate negotiations on long-term dangers.

(4) Representation on boards of directors: A 1973 act provided employee representation on the boards of all companies employing more than twenty-five workers. Employee representatives have voting rights. Fearful of becoming hostages to management, unions gave this legislation low priority, but they have found board seats a useful source of information.

(5) Expanded collective bargaining: The most far reaching single measure was the Employee Participation Act (Medbestämmandelagen - MBL) which went into effect in 1977. Its provisions oblige the employer to provide the union with continual information about production, personnel policy, and the economic status of the company; the union has the right to inspect the company's books. The law strikes down the concept of managerial prerogatives: all managerial decisions, from hiring managerial personnel to making new investments, are subject to collective bargaining. Moreover, management is required to initiate negotiations with the union on all major changes prior to implementing them. Finally, the union's interpretation of contractual provisions concerning worker influence and employee rights is binding until the labor court rules to the contrary.

(6) Pension fund investment: The largest single source of new capital in Sweden is the Supplemental Pension Fund, which is a contributory pension plan supplementing the basic social security pension, as company pension plans do in the United States. (Unlike American company plans, it encompasses all workers and allows employees to move freely from one firm to another without losing pension rights.) It

seats public representatives on boards of directors
when its shares entitle it to a seat. (By contrast,
company pension funds in the United States are
usually company controlled and generally managed by
banks and insurance companies; putting public representatives on company boards is not among their
priorities.) Still on the drawing board is the controversial proposal for a wage-earner fund, which
would divide the growth in invested capital between
employees and shareholders. The current proposal,
drawn up by a joint Social Democratic-trade union
working group, calls for converting 1% of the wage
sum of each company and 20% of its excess profits
(defined as profits over a limit, suggested to be 15
to 20% of risk capital) into employee share capital
invested in the company. At that rate, the wage-
earner funds would gain a dominant interest in the
Swedish economy over a fairly short span of years,
starting with the most profitable firms first.

THE WHOLE IS GREATER THAN THE SUM OF THE PARTS

No single one of the Swedish work life reforms is
revolutionary. Most of the measures are unexceptional
. . . individually. Other nations have gone farther
in a variety of areas. German workers hold half the
seats on corporate boards, and have done so in the
coal and steel industry for three decades. Some of
the American "humanization of work life" projects are
far more radical in terms of job redesign. A few
French and Italian judges have taken to putting
employers in jail for manslaughter when fatalities
occur in industrial accidents. That the Swedes have
become the model for democratizing work life is not a
result of the radicalism of any single Swedish reform,
but of the comprehensiveness, scope, and cumulative
impact of an interlocking group of reforms. Taken as
a group, the Swedish measures constitute a fundamental
attempt to restructure authority relationships in the
economic sphere, to replace the pattern of managerial
absolutism established during the industrial revolu-

tion with a different, more democratic pattern. To list the measures undertaken is, in a way, misleading, for the whole is greater than the sum of the parts.

One cannot visit many Swedish plants without realizing that the reforms of the last decade have had a cumulative impact on plant management and on the shop floor. Managerial practices that were the norm ten years ago -- secrecy in decision making, narrow patterns of discussion, little notice before carrying out major changes -- are virtually extinct today, though you sometimes find them persisting in small or foreign-owned firms. A far more open, more democratic style has taken its place. To put it bluntly, plant managers have a new constitutency: their employees. It is a constituency that is far more knowledgeable -- and far closer -- than stock-holders. Today the plant manager is responsible not only to the company president (and thus, indirectly, to the board), but he is also responsible to his employees. Employee goals certainly do not take precedence over those of the stockholders at the company level, but they have substantial weight at the plant level.

To some on the Left, the Swedish reforms seem a sophisticated form of co-optation, a clever manage-rial ploy to incorporate unions in management. And for many employers, the push for workers' influence on the job is just a covert form of socialization, the more insidious for its democratic aura. Who is right?

The reforms actually are consistent with the Scandinavian Social Democratic practice of "func-tional socialism" - the socialization of some func-tions of ownership without transferring the title of ownership. The privileges of ownership are con-ceived as a bundle of rights which, far from being indivisible, can be split in a variety of ways between management and labor. Among those that affect employees collectively, some, like overseeing the day-to-day operation of the firm, remain the province of management; others, like health and safety issues, have become the domain of the employees; and a variety

22

of important decisions (on investment, new products, managerial personnel, and the like) have passed from being managerial prerogatives into an arena of debate, discussion, and collective bargaining. Though management generally retains the right to make the decision in the end, the process of discussion and bargaining frequently has substantial impact on the form that decision takes. In important areas that affect employees individually, the rights of ownership have been carefully circumscribed by rules that not only limit arbitrary firings but also force management to plan production to minimize layoffs.

Increasing workers' influence on management changes some of the rules of the game. It alters the behavior of supervisors, plant managers, company investment planners, and union officials alike. There is little doubt that it is gradually changing their attitudes as well. The lines of class conflict, once so clear in the plant, have become a bit blurred around the edges. The unions have traded the clarity of the old adversary relationship for influence and the compromises that it entails. It is likely that employee influence will, over the long run, reduce the rate of return on share capital; the resulting shortage of private investment capital will increase the need for collectively owned capital. And so, in a way, both radicals and conservatives are correct: co-optation and back door socialization are both parts of the process.

Ultimately it is hard to generalize about the impact of the industrial democracy reforms. Their aim, after all, was a profound decentralization of influence in every company, every plant, every department. The questions at issue vary from shop to shop: at one plant it is acquiring new equipment, at a second, designing a new building; at a third, hiring a new department manager; at a fourth, how to deal with a three week layoff. As in any bargaining situation, the outcome depends on the competence of the opponents. As Social Democratic Prime Minister Olof Palme put it in 1974 at the Congress of the building trades union, "The new laws will open opportunities for blue and white collar workers that were previously denied them. But whether they can and do use these new opportunities is up to the employees themselves."

Interior of the Helsingør shipyard, 1897

COMPARATIVE INDUSTRIAL RELATIONS

Comparing Scandinavian and American industrial relations, like every other comparative exercise, is fraught with pitfalls. But such comparison offers both insight and new ideas if a sensible framework for comparison can be developed and utilized. What criteria are appropriate here?

In any comparative exercise the first problem is how to delimit the subject and draw geographical boundaries around it. In this respect Scandinavian-American comparisons both pose particular problems and offer particular opportunities for fruitful study. Obviously one is interested in investigating differences and similarities between countries, but how different or how similar should these countries be? On the one hand, it might be argued that one should choose neighboring societies which share certain characteristics such as those of geography, language, and cultural history, so that the explanation of differences between them can be narrowed down to a limited number of factors. On the other hand, this argument can be countered by an opposing one: if societies are sufficiently remote from one another, then any similarities between them can be more plausibly attributed to common causes than to mutual influences.

In the case of Scandinavian-American comparisons, there are a number of challenging opportunities. In the first place, within the Scandinavian group of countries, one can seek to identify differences and similarities against the background of certain shared characteristics. Second, one can then make comparisons between each of the countries separately and the United States, taking into account similar and dissimilar aspects of their economic, political, and cultural contexts. It could be argued that there is finally a third stage where one attempts to abstract from the complexities of the three Nordic countries a "Scandinavian Model" and from the heterogeneity of the North American continent an "American Model." Some of those at the conference felt that this latter stage was an illusive goal, while others by the end did feel that they had some idea of models which could guide their understanding.

A second problem is deciding exactly what the actual subject matter for study is. In industrial relations, both among practitioners and academics, there is a tendency to concentrate on how employers, employees, and their respective organizations negotiate with each other to produce rules governing work and employment relations. Such a focus on the representative institutions and formal rules of the labor market is appropriate. But it is not sufficient, certainly where comparisons are made between countries. Such an exercise requires much greater attention to the contexts of industrial relations. This means looking at a number of environmental factors: social and cultural influences; the organization of labor markets; and the ideological and political scene, including the role of political parties and state intervention. For example, one topic to which the conference kept returning was how, in contrast to the Scandinavian countries, the lack of a social democratic or labor party affects American unions and industrial relations.

The comparative study of industrial relations means going beyond the formal institutional pattern of relationships and looking at how social and cultural factors affect more informal aspects of work relations. Thus, for example, it is necessary to try to investigate differences in attitudes towards work, authority, cooperation and conflict between countries. This should not just be done contemporaneously: comparative study requires not just a snapshot at one point in time, but also the consideration of industrial relations systems in their historical contexts. Too often comparisons are made between institutions, relationships, or sets of rules because they share a common name or a rough parallelism. In reality they should only be compared in terms of the functions they perform within each national context. One cannot make a simple comparison between the activities of the AFL-CIO and the national labor federations in the Scandinavian countries. Nor can one easily compare union locals in the United States with union clubs in Sweden. In the context of different collective bargaining structures and the existence of different mechanisms for obtaining benefits, each may fulfill the function for which they were intended and still in practice be very different. To take another example, one must be very careful when comparing the American collective contract with its Scandinavian equivalents. The former is very detailed, lengthy, explicit, and suited to a legalistic and adversary system of industrial relations. In the Scandinavian countries, on the other hand, there is much greater scope for broader agreements and more informal understandings reflecting a less legalistic and possibly more cooperative industrial relations environment. Yet both perform their respective functions for the parties concerned.

A third problem of comparative analysis is how to assess or measure the relative performance of institutions between countries. For American trade unionists visiting Scandinavia there is often considerable admiration (and justifiably) for the various processes (collective bargaining, board representation, legal rights, political channels) whereby Scandinavian workers obtain benefits. Some of these benefits can be quantified and compared, e.g., working hours, standard of living. However, with other matters, it is often difficult to decide whether unionized American workers, through their strong locals, have more or less control over, and participation in, many work-related decisions than do Swedish workers, for example, through their union clubs, works councils, and board representatives. This would seem to lead to the conclusion that it is fruitless to try and decide which set of institutions and behavior is the "best": each has its own special set of problems and opportunities and one may perform better in one respect than in another.

There are a number of stages in the comparative analysis of industrial relations. The first stage is concerned with what might be called foreign industrial relations. This is the study of other countries industrial relations systems in and of themselves. The second stage is the genuine comparative study of industrial relations, where one goes beyond setting countries side-by-side and proceeds to the comparative analysis of topics horizontally across countries. The third stage, which was achieved at the end of the conference, is the development of a perspective on international industrial relations. This is the study of industrial relations in the context of the international economy and of institutions and phenomena which cross national boundaries. This stage has become increasingly important not only because of the activities of supranational agencies, such as the European Economic Community, but also because of the crucial importance of multinational companies. This aspect of industrial relations is to be placed against the background, at the same time, of growing interdependence between countries, intensifying competition, and increasing calls for protectionism in some countries. One topic discussed at the conference was the problems and prospects for international trade union cooperation, such as in dealing with multinational companies in the automobile, electrical appliances, and communications industries.

What is the value of comparative study? First it aims to understand not only foreign systems, but also to develop a better understanding of one's own society. This should develop through looking at similarities and differences and through understanding the relativity of one's own country's system. This should prevent falling into such fallacies as: "How quaint they are," "How wrong they are," "How much better than us they are," or even "It's the same the whole world over, isn't it?"

Second, the potential value of comparative study is to determine whether it might be advisable or feasible to borrow institutions from abroad. It may, of course, be fruitless to attempt to transfer institutions from one society in which they appear to have succeeded to another. Institutions are part of a total context and the consequence of change in one aspect of a system depends on the relationship between all elements of the system. Since these relationships will not be similar between various societies, the effects may be as different as between the differing settings. However, this does not mean that by visiting and studying other countries one cannot develop ideas and goals which can be placed on the agenda in one's own country. The objective then must be to mobilize forces around them and to seek to develop them along lines suitable to one's own country.

Finally, by studying other countries comparatively, one can identify possible future problems and trends in one's own society. This is not to suggest that all societies are developing through similar stages or are becoming more alike. But problems and opportunities develop in different societies at different times and in this respect can be some guide to future trends in one's own society.

– Howard F. Gospel

A Different Industrial Reality
OBSERVATIONS IN SWEDISH PLANTS

The reality of modern industry provides the context for the push for safer, cleaner, and more democratic workplaces. The plants we visited -- a ball
bearing plant, an auto assembly plant, a foundry and
engine plant, and a repair yard and ship motor factory -- are characteristic of the large industrial
plants that form the backbone of the Swedish economy.
Still, they are not typical in every way. Each has a
stronger than average union local with competent,
innovative and frequently controversial leadership.
Moreover, there are obvious and major differences between large plants like these and small, family-owned
firms. The plants we saw compete on the international
market. They are dependent on international demand,
and given the relatively high Swedish labor costs,
they have to match or outstrip their competitors in
terms of innovation in production technology. It is
a harsher competitive environment than that of the
domestically oriented firm.

Still, the issues raised in the plant visits are
relevant elsewhere -- and not only in industry but
also in white collar and service occupations which
are often ignored in discussions of automation and
technology. Swedes have moved away from the narrow
focus on nominal wages and toward participation in
the organization of work and in making jobs more
pleasant. The unions and Social Democrats look
toward an employee share in ownership as well. The
increased emphasis on these issues has come from both
the union leadership and from the shop floor. Such
concerns are not restricted to labor relations
"experts," but evident in the demands of trade union
locals. Moreover, the importance of quality of work-

ing life issues is underlined by the rise in absenteeism and the difficulty in recruiting labor for monotonous, dull, and dirty -- but well paid -- work.

The barrage of new legislation in Swedish industrial relations is impressive: the Act on Employee
Representation on Boards of Directors (1973 and 1976),
the Act on Security of Employment (1974), the Act on
the Status of Shop Stewards (1974), the Working
Environment Acts (1974 and 1978), and the Act on
Employee Participation in Decision-Making (effective
1977). While conceived at the height of the boom of
the late 1960s and early 1970s, these acts have been
implemented in the context of a political swing right
in 1976 when the Social Democrats lost power after 44
years in government and in the midst of the economic
troubles that have been common to nearly all Western
economies since the mid-1970s. Declining export competitiveness, sluggishness in the economies of foreign
customers, and severe sectoral problems (most notably
in shipbuilding and in steel) do not provide a propi-
tious atmosphere for reform.

Technological, legislative, and economic changes
have a sharp impact on the shop floor.

• The demands for greater productivity have
accelerated the pace of technological change. International observers have long remarked on the relatively
positive attitude of Swedish labor unions toward automation and changes in work procedures. We were anxious
to see if this attitude would continue at a time of
rising unemployment.

• Swedish innovations in work procedures have replaced the traditional assembly line with more flexible
and, some would suggest, more humane procedures. The
factory visits allowed us to see the alternatives in
practice and to discuss the impact with the workers
and their representatives.

• Recent Swedish legislation has allowed employees
to gain entry to the management process and to participate in decision-making. Measures currently under
discussion may alter the forms of ownership not in
the direction of "state nationalization," but in
regional capital funds. Employee attitudes toward

these issues and opportunities were explored on several of the factory visits.

● Swedish occupational health and safety legislation places primary responsibility for enforcement not on government regulators but on safety stewards and safety committees in the plant. How does this work in practice?

● Some major Swedish industries – most notably shipbuilding – face American-size problems with retrenchment and plant closings. We were interested in seeing how they dealt with these questions.

The plant visits, therefore, were arranged to give American observers a first hand view of Swedish industrial reality through discussions with employees, with their unions, and with management. Here is a brief account of what we saw and heard.

GÖTAVERKEN SHIPYARDS, GOTHENBURG

The Götaverken Shipyards were chosen for a visit for several reasons. The shipyards have been the largest individual places of employment in Swedish industry. They expanded rapidly in the 1960s as management found a specialty in the shipbuilding industry suitable to Swedish conditions. That specialty was oil tankers, and at various Swedish shipyards along the country's west coast some of the world's largest tankers were constructed. By specializing in one major product, Swedish shipyards were able to apply the latest engineering and construction techniques. Götaverken in particular was famous for its "assembly line" method of ship construction, where sections of new ships moved along a track for more rapid assembly.

Although this specialization proved initially to be a very profitable idea, given Sweden's relatively high labor costs (even compared to other European shipyards), it made the industry vulnerable to the dislocations that followed the oil crisis of 1973-74. As demand for high-priced petroleum stagnated, orders for the large tankers dried up. Simultaneously the competitive pressures of lower cost shipyards intensified. Japan had long been a keen competitor, but now pressures were added from South Korea, Brazil, and other "New Industrial Countries." From a peak of nearly 24,000 employees in 1975, the workforce in Sweden's shipbuilding industry has declined to about 13,000. An additional 4,500 jobs are expected to disappear in the next 18 months.

When the crisis in the shipbuilding industry became apparent in the late 1970s, the Swedish government (a coalition of non-socialist parties) commenced a policy of subsidies and state take-overs. Over two billion dollars have been spent trying to prop up and convert the industry. Ironically more of Swedish industry was "nationalized" in the first five years of non-socialist government than in the preceding 44 years of socialist rule; this was another example of the common European phenomenon: "lemon socialism," or state support for declining industries.

As the center of shipbuilding, Sweden's second city of Gothenburg was especially hard hit, with the loss of 8,000 jobs in the yards and 3,000 more among suppliers and subcontractors. Of the four shipyards in Gothenburg, two were closed, one converted to a new specialty: support rigs for offshore oil and gas drilling, while the yard we visited, Götaverken's City Yard, has specialized in ship repair and conversion. The local metal workers' union, which organizes nearly all shipyard employees, had to protect their members' interests under particularly harsh conditions. The local union leadership has thus had several concerns. First, as lay-offs increased, there was concern for finding alternative employment for both skilled and unskilled workers. Given Sweden's extensive national employment and training program, the basis was already in place. In response to union pressure, the legislation providing for the rationalization of the ship construction industry contained exceptional provisions for additional job locating and retraining services. Local union officials felt that, given the massive lay-offs, they were very successful in finding adequate alternative employment. Some of the American trade unionists on the visit noted that the burden seemed to have been shifted

SHUTTING DOWN SHIPYARDS: "THE PROBLEM IS ECONOMICS"

Gothenburg has been a shipbuilding town for generations. As recently as eight years ago, its four major yards made it one of the premier shipbuilders of the world. But the Gothenburg yards, which specialized in mammoth oil tankers, were hard hit by the international crisis. In 1975 they employed 14,000. Today 6,000 are left.

Under the Employee Participation Act, the local union was deeply involved in making decisions about the contraction, and it was roundly criticized for its complicity in the layoffs.

What difference did union influence make? Chief shop steward Inge Carlsson: "The problem is economics. You can't change that by passing a law. Let me free you from your illusions: our economic system functions just like yours, though perhaps not so brutally." Still the union's board seats and legal right to full information and negotiation of every major decision enabled them to play a significant role in encouraging alternate production for the hard-hit yards. The Arendal yard, located in the outer harbor, has been converted to building offshore platforms and is currently negotiating the purchase of an English construction firm involved in North Sea development that would expand its access to the field. A floating factory project for Persian Gulf countries that would convert natural gas -- currently flared -- to fertilizer is in the financing phase. The diesel motor division, which is the major supplier of motors for the remnants of the Swedish shipbuilding industry, is working on a wind generation project for Hawaii. The City yard in the inner harbor survives as a repair yard. This is a good thing, for in 1982 for the first time in this century no new ships will be built in Gothenburg.

Even with this considerable success in conversion, 8,000 jobs disappeared in the shipyards in the last six years as two of the yards closed completely, and the other two cut their employment. Much of the reduction came through normal attrition, but ultimately that was not enough.

The union was actively involved in the reductions in force. Swedish law provides that lay-offs follow seniority, but following the law, given the magnitude of the cuts, would have meant firing all younger workers. "The final result would have been the liquidation of the yards, not a stronger firm prepared to deal with the new, competitive environment," says Carlsson. When the yards were nationalized, the government undertook a rationalization of the industry, while giving employees a two-year guarantee of employment.

The union rejected the overmanning of the yards that this implied. Instead, it bargained for -- and got -- the creation of a massive retraining and alternate production project, "Project 80," which absorbed all excess workers. Project 80 offered job retraining, academic courses, and a variety of special development projects designed to develop new products that could be produced in the existing facilities, and whatever part of the project an individual worker was involved in, he drew the same pay he had in the shipyard for two years. Of the 1300 manual workers transferred from the yards to Project 80 -- and they were presumably those with greatest difficulty in finding new employment -- 41% were hired by other firms, 21% were rehired by the shipyards (which were required to give preference in hiring to those in Project 80), 10% took early retirement, and the remainder were drawing sick or disability pay at the end of the project in January 1981. "Whatever our faults," underlines Carlsson, "not one of our members ended up on the unemployment line."

from those who previously had held jobs to those just entering the labor force who otherwise would have found jobs. This impression is partly confirmed by Swedish statistics that show a disproportionate burden of unemployment on new entrants to the job market (youth and women).

A second concern for the local metal workers' union was insuring the best possible economic and working conditions for those whose jobs were saved. Given the centralization of basic wage negotiations (at the national LO -- confederation -- and national metal workers' union levels), local variation was limited. During a period of national economic recession and a sectoral crisis in shipbuilding, wage negotiations become exceedingly complex. The government has tried to relieve some of the inflationary pressure on wages by reducing income taxes. There has been a complex mixture of policies which in the view of many union leaders has tended to benefit higher income groups more than lower income groups. Although Sweden has thus far resisted the policies of extreme "supply side economics," there is an effort to reduce marginal rates of taxation, which can exceed 50% even for average industrial workers. It was the effort to protect wages that contributed to the breakdown of collective bargaining in the spring of 1980 and the brief strike and lock-out which shut Sweden down for ten days.

The struggle for higher wages remains a fundamental concern for trade unionists in Sweden as elsewhere. What is distinctive about Swedish unionists is their sensitivity to other non-monetary issues. This includes employment security, job safety, so-called "quality of working life" issues, and the international competitiveness of their industries. Rarely are protectionist views displayed in the Swedish metal industries, which must export the larger share of their production. There was, however, some dismay at the challenge of competing with the "New Industrial Countries" and their much lower production costs. This theme would be echoed at each of the Swedish factories on our itinerary.

Despite the pressures on their industry, we found that the union local at Götaverken was also concerned with issues of co-determination and work improvements. The restructuring of the Swedish shipbuilding industry, the largest industrial conversion project in Swedish history, has been drafted through tripartite negotiations: representatives from the unions, management, and the government. In fact, the planning was even more multilateral including not only the national government but also local governments. Management represented private owners in the first phase but state owners later. Creditors were also involved. Although Swedish laws make unilateral plant closing decisions more difficult, the response to the shipbuilding sectoral crisis was not merely in response to legislative requirements. There was a broad consensus that communication and collaboration between management and union was a sensible and natural procedure. That did not imply automatic agreement.

To those less familiar with heavy industry a shipyard is an impressive installation. Everything is built to a giant scale. Engines the size of several houses, steel plating many yards across, cranes soaring skyward all contribute to the sense of industrial strength and sophistication. The investments in capital and human know-how are enormous. Yet it is an industry in sharp decline in most western industrial countries.

The Swedish approach to sectoral decline has been costly in monetary terms, but the impact on employees, their family, and their community has been buffered. Tentatively, a rationalized and reduced shipyard industry has emerged. The new specialization in ship conversions and repair as well as the promising field of offshore drilling and service installation may prove profitable. It will be years before an answer can be given. At Götaverken the attitude of the union is one of "cautious optimism" -- a view quite compatible with the Swedish temperament.

SKF, GOTHENBURG

SKF, the Swedish ball bearing company, is typical

MAKING BALL BEARINGS -- THEN AND NOW

SKF-Gothenburg, 1916

The "E" plant, SKF-Gothenburg, 1974

of another form of Swedish industrial enterprise:
the firm that capitalizes on a technological break-
through - the self-aligning ball bearing - to become
a multinational giant, producing and selling only a
small part of its volume in Sweden itself. With the
protection of patents, precision in manufacturing and
stringent quality control, SKF became a dominant force
in the world market.

The basic principle of the ball bearing has evolved
little in recent years. The company has sought to
protect its competitive position (as patents expire
or variant bearings compete in the market) by keeping
production costs at a minimum. It has followed two
strategies. First, foreign plants have been built to
assure access to main markets: the U.S.A., the
European community, and, increasingly, the Third
World. Secondly, plants in Sweden have been modern-
ized to keep costs low and productivity high. Both
of these strategies have consequences for industrial
relations.

Since ball bearing production represents a relatively stable technology, it is suitable for disper-
sal to local plants where costs and marketing conditions are most favorable. This follows the "product
cycle" model whereby multinational corporations can
"scan" the globe for favorable locations. There has
been considerable pressure on Swedish companies
especially in recent years to disperse their production to foreign plants. Most have followed the pattern
exhibited by SKF; foreign plants have been established,
but substantial production remains in Sweden. Non-
economic considerations may play some role in the
decision to remain at home, but hard managerial factors have been decisive. By modernization of plants
and changes in work rules home costs have remained
competitive.

At SKF we were able to see the means toward
remaining competitive at SKF's new "E-fabriken" (E
Factory). This sleek plant was built in 1971-72 to
meet new technological and environmental requirements.
Its 15,000 square meter (approximately 160,000 square
feet) area is arranged to allow continuous production

EMPLOYEE INFLUENCE AT AN AUTOMATED MULTINATIONAL

SKF, the Swedish ball bearing manufacturer, is one of Sweden's most successful companies. The metal workers' local in the home plant in Gothenburg, organized six months after the company was founded in 1907, is also one of the country's most successful. It has a tradition of militance and of competent, sophisticated leadership. It also has substantial influence on management. Two union representatives, including local metal workers' chairman Göran Johansson, sit on the company board, and the union representatives have weekly meetings with plant management that take up every question from wages to long-term investment decisions. The union has achieved virtual veto power over middle management appointments; no one has been appointed in the last ten years without union approval.

It needs all the influence it can get to deal with an automated multinational, says Göran Johansson. New technology has cut the number of jobs in the Gothenburg plant, and the process is continuing. "The company is putting in a new, highly automated line. We have negotiated an agreement with them requiring that it should be manned by blue collar workers, not white collar personnel. We will negotiate questions of training and of the direction of work." The union pushed a program of job redesign with skill expansion and job rotation when the state-of-the-art "E plant" was put into operation in 1973, only to meet opposition not only from management but from members. "When we came and told them, 'we want to make your job more interesting,' a lot of members replied, 'Don't bother me! I'm here to earn money.'"

SKF opened its first foreign plant in 1912, five years after the company was founded. "The question of building plants abroad for SKF is not whether SKF should choose between exporting to the new countries or building plants there. The only way to get into those markets at all is by starting factories," explains Johansson. Wages at West

German and American subsidiaries match those in
Sweden, but French wages lag by 10 to 15% and
British wages are only 60% of the Swedish level.
Wages elsewhere -- in India, Brazil, Mexico,
Argentina, South Africa -- are far lower. SKF does
not propose to supply the Swedish market from
Brazil, but wage levels abroad, particularly in
Third World countries, are a matter of concern.
"We've developed fairly good cooperation with union
locals in foreign plants," says Johansson. "Our
principle is that the cost of international union
work ought to come out of production. And the com-
pany does foot the bill for annual visits to other
European plants. They covered the costs for a union
visit to the Brazilian plant two years ago." The
Swedish local supported the local at SKF's Indian
plant through a successful strike several years ago.
In part because of union pressure, SKF was the first
Swedish company to recognize a black union in South
Africa. "We've been careful in what we have
demanded of management [about South Africa] since
then," says Johansson. "We don't want to impose our
views on other unions. But we do back up their
demands. The most important thing we can do here
is to neutralize company resistance."

Just how much influence does the union have?
"We are moving toward more influence," says
Johansson. "But we have a tendency to look at what
has been achieved as natural and to sense that we
are very far behind in relation to our demands. I
think those active in the union feel they have influence, but I'm not sure that those who come and
just do their job feel the same way .... We and the
company live in an unhappy marriage, but we know we
can't get a divorce. So we have to make the best
of it."

along five highly automated production lines. Special attention has been given to environmental problems connected with ball bearing production. Because of the potential presence of noxious fumes, ventilation has been designed with air inputs in the floor and exhausts in the roof. There are some 7,000 air holes in the floor.

Noise is another potential problem in metal working. Sound-absorbing materials and baffles cover the entire plant with special isolating enclosures built around especially noisy machines. Nevertheless, observers noticed the constant "ringing" of metal parts that is part of the manufacturing process.

Automation and computer control have been extensively employed for efficiency and quality control. Nearly all product movement is along chutes and belts. While heavy physical labor has been largely eliminated, repetitive tasks are common. It is an "assembly line" process, but one refined to a high degree. Machine-assisted human labor has prime responsibility for quality control. The complex manufacturing equipment also requires extensive control and maintenance. Such tasks range from repetitive routine to great variation.

The firm's emphasis on advanced technology and high quality means that employee training is extensive. Such facilities exist on the factory site. Employees also enjoy good facilities for changing, clean-up, and time-off. As is typical of Swedish factories, employees and their unions have had much input into the design of these facilities. SKF has a long tradition of employee and union consultation predating legislative mandates on these matters. The metal workers' union local at SKF is one of Sweden's strongest with a wide range of leisure activities and facilities. Although not unique, the efforts of the union to involve their members illustrates a dimension of labor activism worthy of consideration. First, such leisure time activities create a sense of community. Secondly, many of the program items develop organizational and bargaining skills. Thirdly, the informal contact between members and their union officers and

officials promotes communication and allows problems
to be recognized at an earlier stage. Such facilities,
supported in part by public and company funds might be
difficult to reproduce in foreign settings. Swedish
workers tend to live in reasonable proximity to their
places of employment, even in a metropolitan area
such as Gothenburg. Nevertheless, it is a far from
trivial source of union and employee strength.

The SKF plant is an example of advanced technique
but relative product stability. Ball bearings do not
change much from year to year. SKF owns and organizes
the production process from basic manufacturing
materials (high-grade steels) through the recycling
of waste materials. It has sought to disperse its
manufacturing so as to guarantee access to its vital
foreign customers and to take advantage of different
national cost conditions. Management and union seem
satisfied at the balance between home and foreign
production. Contributing to this mutual satisfaction
has been a long tradition of labor-management cooperation and collaboration.

SAAB AUTOMOBILE ASSEMBLY PLANT, TROLLHÄTTAN

Some fifty miles northeast of Gothenburg lies
Saab's principal passenger car plant. Saab is a
highly diversified industrial concern making cars,
trucks (Scania), computer equipment, and aircraft.
The firm began as an aircraft manufacturer (Saab
means Svensk Aeroplan Aktiebolaget -- Swedish Aircraft
Corporation) and became a major passenger car pro-
ducer only after World War II. To some it is remark-
able that a country of eight and a half million can
support two independent automobile companies. Despite
extensive private automobile ownership in Sweden,
export markets take the majority of cars produced in
the country. Saab has traditionally sought its own
"niche" in the world automobile market. Its earlier
cars emphasized unique engineering and safety considerations before the latter became common policy.
The aerodynamic profile and two-cycle engine gave the
cars a "nonconformist" image. Sweden's transformation to a high-cost country and foreign competition

compelled Saab to abandon its lower priced cars for the more exclusive product of the last decade.

Changes at Saab have not been limited to new car models. In the 1970s the firm instituted extensive changes in the manufacturing process with important consequences for its assembly employees. These changes were stimulated by a deterioration of labor relations and growing personnel problems that affected much of Swedish industry. Swedish employers had greatly rationalized their procedures during the 1940s and 1950s following the precepts of "scientific management," which - based on the original techniques developed by the American engineer Frederic Taylor at the turn of the century - emphasized the organization of industrial work into high-disciplined but low-skilled tasks. Nowhere was this approach more thoroughly applied than in automobile production.

Swedish industry benefited greatly from the initial stages of work rationalization, but by the late 1960s problems were evident. After twenty years and more of full employment and rising income, Swedish industrial workers began to avoid the less attractive jobs. Better education, travel, and increased political sophistication among industrial workers contributed to the frustration over the widening gap between their regimented worklife and their liberated free time. In addition to recruitment problems for low status jobs, the rate of absenteeism for illness rose from 5-6% in the early 1960s to 15% a decade later. Very high employee turnover (50-120% per year) added to the costs of training and quality control. Although foreign labor was actively recruited to meet the permanent shortage of labor, such policies had high training and social costs. The sum of these problems for Swedish industry was rising costs, falling quality and reliability, and inevitably poor economic results.

Swedish labor union leaders were also aware of the spreading unrest which erupted into wildcat strikes and deteriorating relations between local members and their union representatives. Swedish firms' interest in job redesign was welcomed by most

unions, for there was concern that automation might
be the preferred method of eliminating the dissatis-
fied workers. Historically, Swedish unions have had
a positive policy toward technological change. The
country's elaborate full employment policies provided
the security of new employment for those displaced by
technology. It is perhaps fortunate that the work
reforms commenced during the era of full employment.

One of the most interesting examples of job redesign is Saab's body plant where the production line
has been replaced by "line-out" - self-managed assembly
teams. The reform has two major components. First,
in place of the hierarchical and rigidly supervised
assembly line, where each worker had very specific
and differentially rewarded individual responsibilities, new work groups were organized. Each group has
responsibilities for manufacturing, adjustments,
checking, maintenance, administration, training new
members, and other related tasks. Each group had a
"contact man" who interacted with management in setting plant production schedules and dealt with problems. Within each group job responsibilities rotated.

The second dimension of the "line-out" reform was
the "buffer system," which both union and management
feel has been an essential ingredient of the reform.
Buffer stocks have been established between the production groups. Each piece of work is not delivered
at a preset line tempo, but is available when needed
from the buffer stock. In turn, a group's completed
work goes into a buffer between it and the subse-
quent group. The result is radically increased group
autonomy as each group controls its own production
tempo. The size of the incoming and outgoing buffers
set relatively wide limits for the group production
tempo. If the outgoing buffer is full, the group can
take a break of an hour or more.

Management knew that the buffer system would be
more expensive to maintain, relative to the line,
because it requires both space for the buffers between groups and ties up capital in stock. These
costs have been dwarfed, however, by savings achieved
through more stable production. On the line, exces-

JOB REDESIGN: "IT MAKES AUTHORITARIAN MANAGERS IN-SECURE"

Like other traditional assembly plants, Saab's main auto assembly plant in Trollhättan was plagued in the early 1970s by high rates of personnel turnover and absenteeism that raised costs and cut quality. The body shop -- where auto bodies, doors, trunk and hood lids are assembled, welded, and finished -- was particularly hard hit. In 1970-71 the turnover in the body plant was 78%; management estimated that every new employee cost 8,000 Skr [roughly $2,000].

In an effort to find a way to ameliorate these costly symptoms of worker dissatisfaction, the body shop management and the local metal workers union agreed to a pilot project with group assembly of auto doors in 1971. The pilot project was so successful that in 1975 the main line was eliminated in the body assembly plant. It was replaced by production groups of seven; three teams of two each weld, sand, and adjust the bodies while the seventh in the team performs the functions of the traditional foreman. This last job rotates among the seven on a weekly basis.

From production workers' view, abolition of the line was an unmitigated success. On the line, the average work cycle had been three minutes; now it is forty-five. Initially this made the work itself more interesting, for it demanded greater skill. "When we started, I was proud of my cars," says Ove Johansson, "because it was a demanding job to do all that. And there was some pride in seeing what you had made. After a while it got to be routine again; it's dull when you've got it down pat. But there isn't any question that it beats the assembly line."

What really makes group assembly more interesting today, shop steward Bo Blomberg says, "is the rest of what the group does: training new members, budgeting [each group has its own budget], doing 90% of the repairs on equipment. And you control your own time." This last is crucial, for it allows people to work at their own speed, rather than the speed of the line. The buffers of finished work between the teams permit individuals to take breaks of up to one and a half hours (when the buffer is completely filled) as they choose. Furthermore, the flexibility of team production has permitted setting up a rehabilitation group for those who have been ill or injured, making a place in production for them; thus the workplace assumes some of the obligations for welfare now resting on the government.

For Bertil Andersson, Saab's top manager in the shop, the abolition of the line seemed a risky proposition. "I was convinced that the production line was most efficient. I was surprised when we proved the opposite." Andersson is toughminded when it comes to the bottom line. "We're just like every other car manufacturer. We are not going to use any organization form that is not competitive or better." But ten years of work with job redesign have made a believer of him. "The perfect planning of the industrial engineers [in the Taylorist assembly line] has failed .... The line is simply uneconomical. Sometimes it may be unavoidable, but you should throw it out whenever you can."

But of course the skeptic cannot resist the question: "If all the reforms are so positive, then why were they not pushed earlier?" Roger Svensson, body shop manager, smiles. "Managers are trained to be authoritarian. It makes us feel secure to run things that way. Anybody who believes in order prefers the assembly line over the teams. You go out on the floor and what do you see? A bunch sitting and talking, another group playing cards, others reading, asleep. It's enough to make a manager feel insecure."

sive absenteeism, mechanical breakdowns, and the like
simply shut down the line for shorter or longer
periods. With team assembly, excessive absenteeism
after a holiday means only fewer teams working, not a
problem manning the line. Mechanical breakdowns
affect one group, not the entire assembly line.

The financial savings of the new system are impressive. Production stability and quality are up; labor
turnover and absenteeism are down. The number of non-
productive personnel has been cut by the groups'
assumption of many training, quality control and other
supervisory functions. The company calculates that
it recovered its entire investment in the new facilities in two and a half years, an internal rate of
profit of close to 40% annually, and that the continuing annual gains from production stability alone
exceed the annual costs of line-out by a factor of
five.

The "line-out" method at Saab has had its diffi-
culties, particularly during the initial period.
Some groups have been reluctant to take on women or
older workers who might cut group efficiency. The
financial rewards for greater group responsibility
and greater individual skill are low. The main
"reward" of the new procedures for the assembly
groups is much greater control over their working
pace and the opportunity to "earn" longer breaks
during the working day. Some groups have had internal
personality conflicts, a problem less likely to occur
under the old assembly line. None of these problems
has been severe and while refinements of the "line-
out" method may continue, a return to the old system
is inconceivable to union or management. Although it
may be difficult to assess the factors behind the
improved absenteeism and labor turnover – some of the
improvement surely is due to much tighter job opportunities during the past eight years – there is no
doubt about the financial results for the company or
the attitude of employees.

Observers of the Trollhättan plant are usually
impressed by the superior working conditions compared to the standard automobile body plant. By

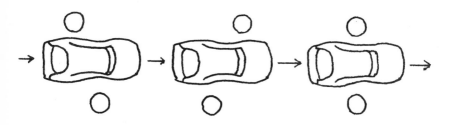

The traditional line in the body shop; work cycle about three minutes

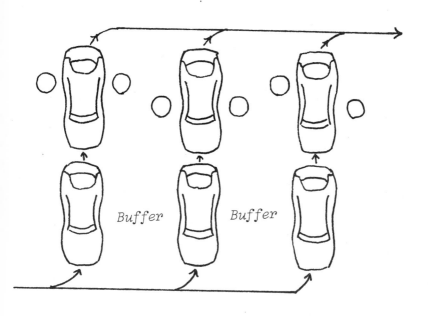

The "line out" system; work cycle about forty-five minutes

American standards the plant is small and the product expensive. While many of the principles of group assembly could be applied in larger plants, American observers believe that management will prefer to substitute robots and CAM (computer-aided manufacturing) for workers wherever possible given the scale of American production. There is some of this at Saab too. It will be a close race between efforts to improve the efficiency, quality, and desirability of assembly work and the substitution of machines for people.

The group method visible at Trollhättan and in fact at many other factories in Sweden raises additional questions. Is not the principle of group self-management a reform suitable for many different working environments? Office, service, and communications workers are often just as tied to hierarchical assembly line type work environments as the traditional automobile worker. These jobs too are being changed radically by technology. It will be a challenge to work reform to apply the advances made in one area to another. The Saab example gives inspiration but no immediately applicable formula.

VOLVO FOUNDRY AND ENGINE PLANT, SKÖVDE

Sweden's other automobile company, Volvo, also produces a wide range of related products. In addition to its automobiles, Volvo makes marine engines, trucks, and farm and earth-moving equipment. It is both an older and larger car company than Saab, but it too is dependent on export markets. Like Saab, Volvo was motivated toward work reform by the problems of finding, training, and holding workers in lower status jobs. Volvo instituted large scale changes both in the organization of work and in making traditional tasks less unpleasant.

Volvo's foundry in the small industrial city of Skövde used to be considered old and unpleasant by Swedish standards. Most foreign observers would find it considerably above their norms for plants of similar function today. The old plant was retro-fitted to meet modern health and safety standards, a process American companies often claim is too expensive. There are, of course, limits to how pleasant a foundry can be. Heat, vapors, and dust are inseparable from the process. Precisely because of the potential hazards, there is much to be won in safety and environmental improvements. The experience at Skövde demonstrates that such policies are compatible with efficient production and inseparable from organizational efforts to improve working conditions.

Swedish laws regulate occupational health and safety (OHS) in three ways. First, the law requires management to employ experts in occupational health and safety, including engineers, medical doctors, nurses, and other professional specialists. These people attend not only to the daily maintenance of OHS, but seek ways of improving conditions. Preventive measures enjoy, naturally, strong support among OHS professionals. Secondly, working conditions must meet stringent national regulations enforced by government inspection. Thirdly, the union and employees have their own staff of safety stewards, employed at company expense, to supervise OHS from the employee's point of view. These safety stewards have the power to stop production and call in state inspectors when they feel such measures are justified. Matters rarely reach such an extreme because there is continuous communication on OHS matters between management and union officials.

Our group was impressed by the attitudes toward and the extent of occupational health and safety measures in Sweden. Few American plants have doctors trained in industrial medicine on their premises full time. Emergency care is frequently adequate, but there is inevitably less professional emphasis on preventive measures. Few American plants match the Swedish norm.

The cost to society of occupational accidents and illness is enormous. Although this is obvious in Sweden where the public sector pays for medical care and disability pensions, it is equally true in countries where such direct costs are met through private insurance or by the employee. The indirect costs of industrial accidents and illnesses weigh heavily on individuals, families, and society. While the direct costs to the firm of cleaning up the workplace are substantial, Volvo recovers a portion through lower rates of sickness and absenteeism. The net social and economic benefits to society far outweigh the expense. Volvo's management seems unconcerned about the impact of these costs on the company's competitiveness, but that is surely related to Volvo's market segment; it sells on quality, not price.

The new engine plant that is part of the Skövde complex has incorporated many of the work reforms we saw at Saab. The standard assembly line has been replaced by team assembly. We observed more restrained enthusiasm at Volvo than at Saab. The novelty of the new system has worn off. Even in the beginning the union's input into establishing the work group system was low, and many local union people feel that management's only interest in job redesign is increasing productivity.

Once again, the race between humanizing jobs and automating them out of existence was obvious. Much of the routine work at Skövde has been automated, and many more sophisticated jobs will be eliminated by new technology in the 1980s. The first robots are on the floor and more will follow.

Even more than Saab, Volvo is an example of a Swedish multinational corporation. The company collaborates closely with several other European car manufacturers and has several foreign assembly plants. An assembly plant was purchased and partially fitted in Virginia to supply the American market, but the collapse of the car market and changing Swedish cost factors have delayed opening the plant indefinitely. Volvo also attempted a complex deal with the Norwegian state (and oil company), whereby Volvo's technological and manufacturing know-how and capacity would be bartered for Norwegian petroleum. After lengthy negotiations approval was won from both Norwegian and Swedish state authorities and the unions, but was finally rejected by Volvo shareholders. Clearly it is a company willing to try the unconventional. Its employees must use their consultative rights to protect their interests.

The Swedish examples are impressive to foreign vistors, especially to Americans who are more used to managers who challenge workers' right to collective bargaining than to those who say they welcome worker participation in managerial decisions. But Swedish unions and employers are obviously not content, and foreign competition continues to provide a strong stimulus for innovation. At both the plants we visited and the national headquarters of the Swedish Metalworkers' Union a similar theme was voiced: "It has worked well up to now, but what of the future?"

That, of course, is not something we can prophesy. Nor is our brief exposure grounds for definitive conclusions. We saw Swedish workers making products we make in the United States. The products and the technology of making them are similar to ours. But work organization, the work environment, and employee input are different. Some of the differences are the consequence of Swedish legislation that requires management to inform, consult, and bargain with employee representatives, but many innovations in the plants we visited predate formal co-determination laws. The unions do have a great deal of input, and management apparently does feel that a more democratic decision-making structure is worth the time it takes because the decisions reached are, if not better, at least carried out with more enthusiasm. It is obvious that the Swedes can compete in the world market despite -- or because of -- their worklife reforms. We import cars built at the Saab plant in Trollhättan. But should we import aspects of the work organization, of the union input into managerial decisions, of the health and safety system used in building them?

SAFETY STEWARDS CAN STOP DANGEROUS WORK

Though occupational health isn't as sexy as abolishing the assembly line, many consider the Swedish occupational health and safety law to be the most important single industrial democracy measure on the books. One of its key provisions is shop floor enforcement by safety stewards, trained by the union on company time, who can order work stopped while pay continues if a job or process is deemed dangerous.

At Volvo's foundry in Skövde, an old plant retrofitted to minimize hazards, that ultimate sanction has never been used in part because of the clout it gives the safety steward. "If a safety steward considers a machine dangerous, he takes it up with the department head. We nearly always get satisfaction at that level," explained Claes Cöran Lundin, head of the Volvo union local. Ten years ago, the Skövde foundry was a dirty, dangerous place to work. Today, says Lundin, "The work environment has been improved to the point that we no longer need major new investments. All that is required now is a bit of vigilance ...."

Much of the credit for the improvement goes to the work of the plant clinic, which is staffed by three doctors specializing in industrial medicine, five nurses, and two physical therapists. While the clinic is funded by the company, union representatives have a majority on the plant health committee that oversees its operation. Moreover, the national contract requires that plant doctors devote at least 50% of their time to preventive medicine, rather than just patching up the damage. During the last four years the clinic has done complete examinations of all foundry employees and the doctors have examined the work environment at each work station together with the shop safety stewards. The doctors also advise on new equipment and on planning new facilities.

The company's technical safety department is also responsible to the union-dominated plant health and safety committee. Its work is governed in part by

the national agreement on health and safety between
the trade union federation and the employers' federation. Safety engineer Lars Erik Lindqvist re-
ported little friction and much cooperation with
union safety stewards. One of his current head-
aches is extracting precise information on the com-
position of chemicals used from the companies that
make them in order to determine what risk they
pose. All that information is shared automatically
with safety stewards, who have a legal right to it.
The problem is extracting it from reticent suppliers.

The system rests on the close cooperation between
company personnel, doctors, and union safety
stewards. Cooperation to improve health and
safety seems noncontroversial. Sweden is a small
country, so the potential victims of industrial
diseases are your neighbors, and the Social Democratic government's bill that froze 20% of Swedish
companies' 1974 profits (which were excellent) to
be released for new investments to improve health
and safety with union consent took the issue out of
politics. Union safety stewards retain the dracon-
ian power of stopping production but it is rarely
used -- roughly 100 times a year in all of Swedish
industry. As one union safety steward put it,
merely mentioning it "makes them marvelously cooperative."

WHAT CAN AMERICANS LEARN FROM SCANDINAVIANS?
A ROUNDTABLE DISCUSSION

The workshop closed in Stockholm with a comparison of the American and Scandinavian situations and a discussion of what - if anything - Americans can learn from the Scandinavian experience.

BOB BUFFENBARGER (INTERNATIONAL ASSOCIATION OF MACHINISTS):
What I saw here in the Scandinavian countries and appreciated is the combination of strong union organization and political activity. Remember the man at Saab who told us that it takes both and he pointed to his two pins [trade union and Social Democratic] that he wore proudly? And Scandinavians are successful in getting good legislation for the unions. On the down side, we both have very serious problems. Management always has the initiative. The union is constantly reacting, adjusting, suffering losses in order to save jobs. And I saw at Volvo yesterday where management is building for twenty years ahead. I never saw any strong projection from the union that they too are looking that far ahead.

The IAM met in New York prior to this trip and it was unanimously decided for contracts coming up in '82 that management rights are going to be challenged, strongly we hope. That is a start.

GEORGE SULZNER (UNIVERSITY OF MASSACHUSETTS [AMHERST]):
One of the things that struck me was that it appears for concrete progress to be made here in labor relations - in whatever field we are talking about whether it is co-determination or the enforcement of work environment laws - the situation is the same as it is in the United States: that is, that you have to get the cooperation of the representatives at the plant level. There is a gap between

what appears at a national level in agreements that were negotiated centrally and the actual working out of those concepts at the local level. There isn't much difference between what happens in the U. S. and Sweden and Denmark in that regard.

BOB JENSEN (UNITED AUTO WORKERS): I think that the strong unions here are really the result of political power on the national scene. I don't think the Swedish unions would have accomplished any of this without controlling the Social Democratic party. And a lot of the changes that were made stem from that. The engineer from the Saab-Scania who sold his idea to the company for the line-out system in the body shop was a product of thirty years of the Social Democratic government. He grew up under that system. That's why he thinks the way he does.

As our union has always said, the ballot box is inseparable from the bargaining table. Anything you gain at the bargaining table you need legislative power to keep. I think that is an important lesson too few of our members take into consideration.

The Swedish labor unions have a real concern about capital investment, a concept we don't talk too much about in the U. S. among labor. They are an export nation and they realize that they - like the Japanese - have got to export to survive. It looks like labor is going to tell management, "If you can't make a profit, get out of business. We are not going to put our money [from the wage earner funds] into an unprofitable organization." There is another difference: in the United States we think that we're independent of the rest of the world; there's still the attitude that we can do it on our own. We have all the food that we need, we have all the resources we need, we have all the raw material we need and we have all the labor force we need so we can survive.

JOHN LOGUE (KENT STATE UNIVERSITY): But didn't the UAW talk about investment levels before? Didn't you try to get the automobile companies to build smaller cars?

BOB JENSEN: Well, there was a push a few years ago. It was one of Reuther's ideas to build a small

car anyway. We do occasionally raise the demand:
"Plow the profits into capital investments, new
machines, tools, and equipment rather than sending
it overseas or giving it all away to the stock-
holders." We raise that cry, but it has never really
become a major issue at the bargaining table.

ED GRAY (UNITED AUTO WORKERS):

One of the important differences between Scandinavia and the U. S. is
that here the workers are not called
upon to share the burden of the
changing technology in the same way
as in the USA. Unfortunately, in
the U. S. that very often means unemployment for the individual
worker, hardship for his family and
very often a drastic loss for the
community in which a business
enterprise or plant has been
located. Consider the impact of
the closing of the Ford Motor Company plant in Mahwah, New Jersey.
That plant was located in that town for about 25
years and most of the workers who previously worked
at the plant moved with the plant from a former
location some 40 or 50 miles distant. There are no
other jobs there; there is no other manufacturing
enterprise worthy of mentioning within a good many
miles. The shortage of mortgage money and high
interest rates really means that the workers who
worked in that plant and bought homes in the area now
find it very difficult to sell their homes and go
elsewhere to look for work; and there is none there.
All of the benefits available for them under various
government programs have run out and they are now at
the end of the road. We are cooperating with Cornell
University to make some kind of a survey to see just
how bad the picture is, but we know it is pretty bad.
It stands in sharp contrast to the way the problems
of unemployment are treated here. For example, in
Gothenburg we saw what the closing of the shipyards
meant to people there. Obviously they have not suf-

fered the way many Americans have suffered during somewhat similar experiences in the last few years.

One other aspect that is very dramatic to me was the emphasis on changing the nature of work in the plants so as to make it somewhat more pleasant, or at least less unpleasant. And I don't even know that that is regarded as a very serious problem by very many unions in the United States right now. We are struggling to maintain any jobs, so working to make jobs more desirable is relegated to second or third priority. In any event it was very interesting that there is such heavy emphasis among unions on how workers live in the plant. Of course that obviously ought to be the case everywhere. I am hoping that we will arrive at that point someday soon in the United States.

Redesigning jobs was one of the recurring themes in the plant visits. There are constraints on how much the nature of work can be changed if the plant is still to make the same product competitively, but those limits still leave a lot of room for changing the nature of work to make it less unpleasant.

ED GRAY: I think that the reaction of most American union people has generally been that job redesign has been a proposition advanced by companies as a means of getting more production and lower costs out of a given operation. There isn't any real serious effort in the U. S. to tailor a job to make it more suitable for a worker's needs. I am very suspicious of the companies' motives. For example, the Ford Motor Company made an offer to the union in the plant in Norfolk, Virginia that they could have the walls and the production line painted in any color that they wanted and they also offered to pipe in music to the plant during the day. That's all well and good, but the workers saw through it as just being an effort to manipulate them. We just have not seen any serious effort corresponding to what now seems to be going on at Saab and Volvo, perhaps other companies here.

Motors dwarf men in Götaverken's motor plant

FRANK EMSPAK (INTERNATIONAL UNION OF ELECTRICAL,
RADIO AND MACHINE WORKERS): We're talking about
plants of a certain amount of production and size in
Sweden. It's not clear to me that it's applicable
to someone who's producing triple that, like many of
the large American automobile plants.

On the other hand, I saw the enrichment of the
jobs in the shipyard where the machinist [in the
motor plant] does more varied jobs than most of ours
do, though he doesn't seem to get increased compensa-
tion for that. It seemed to me to show that it was
possible certainly for that type of expansion of
skills to go on. We can do that. It's not a big
deal like it's maintained in the United States.
You can increase the skill of a person .... One
has to have an interest in it, and that's true in
the automobile industry as well. I think that's
something that is very concrete. From my point of
view seeing that made the trip worthwhile.

I think we also learned that there are limits,

economic limits that people face here. Nobody is going to be able to deal with the unemployment questions here, I think myself, unless we in the United States are able to. [We have to recognize] a closer relationship between the economic needs of our membership and the political situation. We have to have the political strength to deal with high interest rates and other forms of supply-side economics. In that sense, I think Bob Buffenbarger's theory is quite true.

JOHN LOGUE: I don't think there is any question that many of Volvo's and Saab's departures in job redesign are motivated by a desire to increase their profitability by reducing absenteeism and turnover. That again ties back into the Swedish social welfare benefit system and to the full employment policy which makes it possible for people to choose whether they want to work on an automobile line or someplace else because there are other jobs available. So again national policy ties into the local plant level: that's the context and we don't have that context in the U. S.

I might add one thing. When I was at Saab last year, the union was trying to set up what they called a rehabilitation group in the body shop where people who had been sick for a long time or women in the latter months of pregnancy could work at a reduced pace. That was one of their ideas, one of the union's ideas about the advantages of the system. They had never managed to do that in the first five years of their experiments. Ove Johansson [treasurer of the Saab metal workers' local] said Wednesday they had finally set up a rehabilitation group and it seemed to be working well. So there the plant takes over some of the social responsibility that the company otherwise has been dumping on society. People can come back to work earlier; they don't end up going on disability because they have a sheltered work place inside the factory, sheltered in a kind of plant where you couldn't have sheltered workplaces before because you couldn't have those people on the line. The tempo of the line was set. With team assembly you have got more flexibility. Profit's still the motive at Saab, but on the other hand, you can take other priorities into consideration too.

ERIC EINHORN (UNIVERSITY OF MASSACHUSETTS [AMHERST]): Most of the things that we saw seem to be justified not just by social concern but from an economic point of view as well. I think that might be the message, though it may be of less interest to American labor than it is to American management. American management has always assumed that everything you do that seems to be a concession to labor comes out of your pocket. It appears that Saab's experiments have not been costly in a conventional narrow business perspective. They have been profitable. That ought to be of interest to management as well.

One of the things that lies behind Swedish and Scandinavian labor relations as a whole is that there is not the sense of the zero-sum game where one guy loses and another guy wins what the first guy lost. There is a sense that it is possible to find changes and solutions that benefit both sides. Gains are not always equal but at least there is a net gain. That may not always be possible, even in Sweden. And I think the shipyards show that there clearly are limits in an export-oriented economy to how much good will and consensus can achieve.

GEORGE SULZNER: I think we have seen signs also this week of a slight unraveling of the so-called Scandinavian model. We see developing strains between the private sector and the public sector, and a growing tension between white collar workers and blue collar workers. Those tensions have been developed more fully over a longer period of time in the United States. We don't seem to have any answers but I think to some extent the United States experience will be relevant to what is coming to Sweden.

Another recurring theme in the plant visits was the Swedish focus on occupational health and safety. How does that compare to the American situation?

ED GRAY: Based on what we saw in the last few days, the Swedes have gone much further here than the U. S. The number of people on the medical payroll in the Volvo plant [in Skövde] was really impressive. I know of no comparable case in the United States in terms of people employed by the plant – what is it, 3,000 people or 3,100? In any case, it is rare in the U. S. that a plant of 4 or 5 thousand people would have a doctor around the plant premises – one doctor, never mind several of them. They have a doctor who would be available on call, or a doctor to whom they can take someone, but to have one stationed <u>full time</u> on the plant premises is a very rare case in the U. S. so far as I know. Volvo has several nurses on the payroll and that is also most unusual. We have a nurse per shift; that is about what you would normally find. And here there are also people who are specialists in safety and training and who function in a way that is totally foreign to the American scene. I think that is one of the most impressive things here as far as I am concerned.

BOB BUFFENBARGER: On the other hand in most of the industry that machinists are involved with, safety programs <u>are</u> comparable to those here. We have a comparable situation in almost all the locations as far as union representation and company representation go. Of all the systems that we are involved in directly, our safety program is by far the best, where both company and union really work together. We think OSHA [Occupational Safety and Health Administration] has helped. Working environment <u>has</u> improved and our safety devices are better. On medical staffing, the majority of our contacts <u>do</u> provide for proper and adequate medical coverage; even in over-time situations when many work there must be a medical person there.

JOHN LOGUE: Are your medical personnel required by contract to spend a certain amount of their time doing preventive work in the plant, like this doctor we talked to at Volvo who is required to do 50% preventive work? He was actually doing 60%, he said.

BOB BUFFENBARGER: No. As far as preventive

medicine goes, employees have an opportunity for a complete physical every five years. Those who work in areas where noise, sight problems, or anything like that is a potential hazard are given a screening about once every six months. They keep a record so that if there is a problem, OSHA can come in and have a step by step pinpoint of the deterioration.

ED GRAY: We have our health and safety representatives in the plant too, and we have an ongoing program that is far better than anything we had a few years ago, but that still is not comparable in my judgment to having several doctors on the company payroll who are working full time and dealing with all these different problems. I would guess that we would probably have difficulty finding doctors who would go to work on a company's payroll in the U. S. They couldn't make enough money that way.

BOB JENSEN: Most of the plants have a doctor who comes in part time. He's there 4 or 5 hours. A large plant has a couple or three nurses.

At the international union level we have a large group of industrial hygienists and we have a doctor on our staff, but they are servicing a million and a half members. And they get spread out pretty thin. So they delegate more down to the local level where it should be. Our health and safety reps in the plant are highly trained. Volvo has 80 health and safety stewards out there at the Skövde plant. I added together the total amount of time they get in a plant of that size, and it came out to 2 health and safety reps on a full-time basis. We would have one on a full-time basis. Theirs get one week of education, paid for by the company, and ours get two. Their safety steward spends so much time on his job that he can't become an expert in health and safety in general. I'm not sure that that is good or bad. He may be quicker able to spot defective machines, a guard off of a machine, something like that, but does he really have the knowledge to get into the industrial hygiene aspects of the chemicals? Our full-time guy who is highly trained and generally appointed for life unless he screws up becomes a real expert. And from that standpoint we may be a little better. But I agree with Ed. I was surprised at their large staff of doctors, at their preventive emphasis and the things they get into, and at the fact that where the union has dominant vote on the health and safety committee.

FRANK EMSPAK: I've worked with grants from OSHA. In fact, we have one that provides two full-time industrial hygienists at the local level. And there's no question that there are individual plants that have good systems, where we might have sympathetic doctors, and so on. What is different here is that the structure — the legal structure — and areas of responsibility differ completely from what we have.

What I think we can learn from the Swedish model is, first, that the structure here puts the financial responsibility on the company but the activities of the industrial hygienists (which are paid for by the company) are directed by the employees .... to research this or find out that. So there is a whole different financial relationship and authority structure. No industrial hygienist that I know of at a major plant in the United States can undertake a research project to prove that beryllium dust causes cancer and therefore the company's got to get it out. He or she would last about an hour on that job.

The second thing is the ability, the _legal_ ability (not what we've been able to agree locally) of those 80 safety representatives we've been talking about to stop production. The fact of the matter is that there are very few health and safety stewards in the United States who on their own authority can stop production and keep their job. When you get right down to it, if there's something wrong and it's serious, there are very few foremen who can say "all right, we'll stop production while we get OSHA to inspect it." I think that's a very important fact. The Swedes have coupled with it a somewhat more complicated right-to-know formula that we don't have at all.

We have tried to use this work environment legislation directly in our negotiations and we found it to be a help. To me, if you look at the problems we have with chemicals, with asbestos, and so forth, in the United States and the structure of our public health system, I think we can learn a lot – as well as the limitations about what a capitalist system is willing to do. I think it's a pretty good system the Swedes have got, given those limitations.

All the plants visited were modern and fairly highly automated. Despite that, introducing new technology is a current issue -- and a particular headache for the Swedish union locals. Once very favorable toward technological rationalization, they are now ambivalent. Where are those replaced by robots going to find jobs in these days of economic stagnation? And where are there going to be enough jobs created for those new entrants in the labor market?

JIM FISHER (INTERNATIONAL ASSOCIATION OF MACHINISTS): My primary interest in this conference was automation and new technology. I know what we have back in the States and I wanted to come over here and see just what they had. I found they have the same problem over here that we have at home. There is a whole lot of technology coming in, and the people just don't see it. They say that it's not displacing people, that everything will be taken care of by attrition.

Well, we all have to be pretty naive to believe that. Those machines are replacing all kinds of people, and we better become aware of it, and we better start doing something about it. I don't have any answers myself and these people don't have any answers – in fact, they aren't as aware of it as we are back in the States. I think it's time that Europeans become more aware of the problem. And it is time that somebody comes up with some solutions. Everybody knows the problem exists. Now, how do we correct it? Let's have a conference with some solutions, where we talk about the solution and not the problem.

We should take a bunch of people through these

plants and point out to them, that's a robot, that's what it is doing, and this is a robot that's picking it up and doing that, and this is an NC machine and that's the tape. We are just going to be replaced by robots.

JOHN LOGUE: The robot we were standing around yesterday at Volvo replaced 3 employees.

PER ÅHLSTRÖM (SWEDISH METAL WORKERS' UNION): I think that awareness of the new technology taking away jobs is just as high here and in Europe as it is in the U. S. In other countries, Denmark, for example, they have had big strikes, especially in the news-papers, over new technology. They had them in England too.

In Sweden, this is another case where national policy ties in with individual companies' policies. We are very much aware that new technology takes away jobs. What we have tried to do is to limit com-pany profits from eliminating jobs. We've transferred the profits into the public sector and created jobs there.

The machine shop at the sugar refinery in Lyngby about 1912

DEALING WITH TECHNOLOGICAL CHANGE

Holte, Denmark (PAI). Unions must develop their own competency in understanding technological change if workers' interests are to be protected, a Norwegian expert told an international labor seminar here.

Professor Kristen Nygaard of Oslo University described how the Norwegian Iron and Metal Workers, the strongest union in Norway, launched a pilot project in the early 1970s with the state-supported Norwegian Computing Center.

As a result, local trade unionists and computer technicians developed worker alternatives to management plans for introducing new technology. This led to the 1975 Data Agreement between the Norwegian labor federation and the employers federation and a system of "data stewards" on the shop floor.

The Norwegian experience inspired unions and computer experts in neighboring Sweden and Denmark to study ways of involving workers as new technology moved into the workplace. Nygaard believes trade unions in all countries should have their own experts and a "network" to exchange knowledge and experience.

"I agree 100 percent," declared James Fisher, a district organizer for Machinists Lodge 751 at the Boeing Corporation in Seattle, Washington. Fisher, who attended the seminar here, said there's no question of the need for union competency in dealing with new technology. "It is the most serious threat to the American labor movement that I can think of," he added.

Robert Buffenbarger of Machinists Lodge 912, who is chief steward at the General Electric plant in Cincinnati, believes "unions must have a say." Buffenbarger said unions "have to train our own people." Labor needs the counsel of experts, he said, but in America workers tend to distrust academic experts. "You can't fight technology, but you have to control it. There should be an orderly process for introducing it."

Buffenbarger said he was impressed by how Swedish

unions were consulted before new technology was introduced. However, he said, co-determination sounds good, but is not fully working yet. As he saw it, robots and mechanization in Swedish plants led to a net loss of jobs.

Buffenbarger said that when the Machinists' contract with GE comes up in 1982, the union must challenge management's prerogatives. "We have a right to get involved with the new technology."

Fisher felt that unions had to deal with the new technology of cathode ray tubes, numerically-controlled equipment, computers and robots through bargaining and legislation. "They are killing us in electronics and we need knowledgeable people to deal with it." Ten years ago, he related, 100 people were troubleshooting in his unit at Boeing. Today, 15 people do the same work, with computers locating specific trouble in 15 seconds compared to the few hours it used to take one worker.

"I feel the unions have done a very poor job in the U.S. in coping with the problem. The IAM is taking a leading role, but we are way behind," Fisher said. In Sweden and Denmark, Fisher added, workers have been helped by the fact that Social Democratic governments were in power and passed protective legislation. They haven't faced legislation like the Taft-Hartley and Landrum-Griffin Acts, he said--or a Reagan Administration. It is important for American workers to become politically active and elect friendly legislators. "There's no way to stop the new technology, but we are going to have to get our government to come up with plans for people when the machines take over."

As Fisher observed, machines do not pay taxes or buy products.

– Robert B. Cooney

JIM FISHER: Well, I'm going to go right back to Seattle and I'm going to tell Boeing that I want 8% of the profits and Jensen is going back to auto companies and he's going to tell them the same thing, "Hey, you guys are making too much money and you are taking all of these jobs away from us." They'll laugh themselves silly.

What I'm trying to say is that you can't solve this on a company level; this has to be national policy. If you don't have a national employment policy, it's your bad luck.

LARRY KELLEY (INTERNATIONAL ASSOCIATION OF MACHINISTS): That's one thing that you have over

here. Here you are about 80 to 85% organized. You have had your own politicians in office for 40 years. We're only 20 to 25% organized in the United States and that makes a difference in getting the unions to cooperate in order to get laws and get people into office to make sure we do get the laws. If we did, we'd have it made.

PER ÅHLSTRÖM: I don't think you would have it made any more than we do, because this is still a very difficult problem. It's a very difficult problem to transfer the money from private industry to the public sector where you have the needs and where you can create new jobs. That is a problem we haven't solved in this country. I don't know if there is an ideal system, but it is a very difficult task and one of the big problems of the future if we are going to keep full employment.

ED GRAY: However difficult that would seem to be here, it is nowhere near as difficult as in the United States. More than any other group in society, public employees are being made the scapegoat for all the other problems that we have. President Reagan points a finger at them and says "that's where your money is going, where your tax dollar is being wasted," and he's cutting back on all the governmental social and

labor programs including, by the way, OSHA. That's
going to be now probably given the kind of enforcement we had in New York State for so many years when
we had Republican governors who advocated enforcement
of labor laws by "education." There'll be no penalty
imposed on an employer for even deliberately violating
the law; he'll be "educated" to respect the law, the
next time to apply it differently.

In any case, the virulent attacks that are being
made on public employees in the U. S. are hard to
imagine. There's no talk of expanding employment in
the public sector; it's being cut back all the time.
And if the President has his way, it will be cut back
much more drastically in the next two or three years.

*Expanding worker influence on the shop floor in
Sweden has not been an isolated phenomenon. It is
part of a political and cultural context which,
while like the American in some ways, is very
different in others.*

GEORGE SULZNER: One of the highlights of the trip
for me was seeing how the Swedes have developed the
notion in practice - more fully here than in the
United States - that workers are not one dimensional
not just economic factors, not part of the production
facilities. Workers are different than robots. The
workers are people, human beings and can benefit from
a variety of rich experiences. The idea is a product
of the public sector, of the educational facilities.
It seems to me that we are not going to make any progress in the United States until we can turn people
around in this dimension.

JOHN LOGUE: Part of that is a product of the big
Swedish trade union education program, which is
heavily subsidized by the government. Again there is
this interlock between the public sector and the
unions. It's a system where the parts fit together.
Ours isn't.

ED GRAY: We have come very close a couple of
times to getting federal grants or federal allocation
funds for labor education, but so far as I know there

is no money currently allocated for labor education purposes. There is some state money, but no or almost no federal money is available. What we are talking about here in Sweden are regular government allocations, money given to labor education where trade unions are able to receive that financial aid and are able to use in in the form that they believe meets the needs of their members.

DICK GREENWOOD (INTERNATIONAL ASSOCIATION OF MACHINISTS):

I had two major disappointments on this trip compared to when I was over here three years ago. The first is that I detected disillusionment among many people, beginning in Copenhagen when they spent a day telling us about the collapse of the Swedish or Scandinavian model, and then in talking to other people as we traveled around. There is some sort of a disillusionment with the Social Democratic program. And I am disappointed in that because whatever the strains are, it still seems to me very viable and very functional and it doesn't need to be scrapped. It needs to be sold again.

Inherent in that disillusionment is this decentralization versus centralization phenomenon. It may be new in Scandinavia. I gathered that there were two things feeding it. One could be what we call in the U. S. "an arrogance of power": there were 40 some years of the Social Democratic leadership having its way at the top with a failure to communicate, to get down and comprehend what the folks at the local level are talking about. And the other is sort of a generation gap I detect particularly in Sweden. And I think their dissatisfaction is not so much with the system itself, but they see it as a barrier to entry. And a barrier to have input.

The second disappointment I had is that I detected, particularly at Volvo yesterday, the Americanization

of Scandinavian business. In spite of all the cooperative attitudes and all the great programs, I see a
creeping Americanization of attitudes.

But in spite of all that, it still seems to me when
Reagan economics fail - as they will - and we look to
a model to reconstruct the Democratic Party or whatever political reformation is coming, we are still
going to look at the Scandinavian model, because it is
there. It will have to be adapted, adjusted, but it's
there. And so, on that note, I'm optimistic.

JOHN LOGUE: There _is_ a sense of disillusionment
and it is stronger now than it was several years
back. I think it has been growing. The question is,
is it a product of stresses and strains within the
system or is it fundamentally a product of economic
stagnation? Year after year of economic stagnation
imposes stress on all kinds of systems. The Scandinavians have been very successful, relative to other
people, in dealing with these strains. The strains
come from outside, from the international economy.
The Swedes to some extent have made their domestic
economy recession proof. But it's one thing to make
an economy this size recession proof; it's another
thing to insulate it against changes in the world
market.

DICK GREENWOOD: I think that's true and it was
manifest today when we talked to Carl Johan Åberg
[editor of _Aftonbladet_, the Social Democratic daily
paper]. Three years ago when you posed a question
to Swedish trade union officials in that very room we
met in this morning, "Do you accept this thing they
call the Phillips curve, trading jobs for price control?" They said, "absolutely not. We will not accept that." But today Åberg's underlying assumption
was that they have accepted it: he was telling us
that there has to be some way to forego real wage
increases and real income gain in order to avoid
inflation and in order to maintain full employment.
I won't buy that at all.

PER ÅHLSTRÖM: There is a debate going on within
the Social Democratic party right now on how to get
out of this crisis. It is very difficult for a party

73

in opposition to pursue an economic policy. There are always unpopular measures you have to take if you are in government; and if you, as a party in opposition, say "when we get into power we will have to take these measures," then you will make it legitimate for the present government to make those unpopular decisions without making them part of the comprehensive program. And that's what we are so afraid of. It is one thing if you make some unpopular economic decisions as part of a program to get out of this crisis, and it is quite a different thing if you are just making these unpopular economic decisions and don't do anything else because then you just hand over money to the companies.

ERIC EINHORN: To follow up on Dick's point; the Swedish economic security policies that developed from the 1930s on until the 1960s sought to bridge over what they saw as inevitable business cycles. But the system has only so much capacity to bridge the valleys in the cycle, the recessions. What the Swedes are facing now is the result of almost 10 years of terrible inflation and also 10 years of stagnation, for a variety of reasons, some of which are totally out of the control not only for small nations but perhaps of individual large nations as well.

Right now, the deficit on the Swedish national budget is running about 12% of the GNP. If you multiply that in American terms you can imagine the pandemonium you'd get in Washington. The Swedes are more sophisticated and realize that managing the national budget is not like running a grocery store, but still there are limits. Today, the Swedes – who 10 years ago were almost a model of economic morality in the sense of having very few foreign debts and running a very tight ship – are piling up foreign debt at a very rapid rate. It's not a question of months, but I do think it's a question of years how much longer the system can bear this countercyclical effort. Any government in Sweden is going to have to come up with a solution.

ED GRAY: I'm aware that many economists subscribe

to the point of view that wage increases really cause
price increases and the way to control inflation is
to somehow shut off all the wage increases and
depress wages and cut back on the ability of the
general public to consume goods. Unfortunately I
think a great many trade unionists and trade union
leaders also basically accept that proposition. It
is all mixed up and turned around. They are confused about the cause of a lot of our problems in the
U.S.A.

We need some awareness on the part of the trade
union movement of the role that the multinational
corporations and banks now play in the world. The
role of the U. S. banks particularly is an absolute
and total disaster. There is no way small countries
can really come to grips with their problems, unless
other countries are working with them to do something
about the role of these giant corporations and the
international banking community. Yet the number of
trade unions that you find who really understand that
or are really doing something about it is, I am very
sorry to say, very, very small. We have a challenge
to try to make our members and others in the community
understand what has to be done if we really want to
work at solving our problems.

*Labor-management relations in Sweden have tradi-
tionally been somewhat less antagonistic than those
in the United States, perhaps because the Social
Democrats have virtually monopolized political power.
In the 1970s, various forms of co-determination --
most notably the Employee Participation Act
(Medbestämmandelagen - MBL) -- and other forms of
union participation seem to have reduced that
antagonism further by giving workers considerable
influence on some aspects of running industry. But
have the unions achieved real influence in important
areas? Or, on the other hand, does it seem that the
unions are being co-opted by management?*

FRANK EMSPAK: It looks to me like Swedish unions
have more information about certain things than they

had before. Some of it is useful and some of it comes in a form that cannot be used. When it comes down to investing money and the union has a different position on the decision than capital, I didn't see any evidence that they have much co-determination. I can see in a lot of subsidiary areas that there is a lot of influence that is of interest to the union membership, but on the substantive issues that we were addressing earlier affecting the investment policy of the company it struck me that there wasn't a lot of progress being made through co-determination. It looked to me that the company determined and the union cooperated.

PER ÅHLSTRÖM: Some of our members call the law on co-determination "the horn" because you honk it and then they run over you. And in many cases that is exactly the way it has worked. On the other hand, it is very difficult to judge what the effects of this law would have been if it had been employed in a different economic context. The law was passed just before Swedish industry really started to slide downhill. I think that the unions will have more influence and more power in a situation where the economy is growing, where decisions are made on new investments. It is much easier to influence the direction when something is expanding than to have influence on contraction because that is imposed upon you from outside. It is just not the company being against you; it's the whole economy. It is very difficult to say what co-determination could have been in an expanding economy; I think it would have been much more effective.

JOHN LOGUE: To give an illustration to what you were saying: at SKF, Göran Johansson [the chairman of the metal workers' local] commented to me that there had not been a management appointment at the department level that the union had not agreed to. They had blocked several. They have in effect acquired a kind of veto power over appointments, at least at that middle level in management.

BOB JENSEN: But of all the plants, that plant struck me differently than any plant I have ever

76

seen and the nature of the work has a lot do with
union response.

That plant, you might say, is the ultimate
factory. They make five sizes of bearings. The
same bearings were produced 25 years ago and the
same bearings, unless they come up with a plastic
bearing that will never wear out, will be produced
25 or 50 years in the future. A bearing is a bearing
is a bearing. And they have the tooling set up there
and it is going to remain there year after year. I
suppose they used a lot of that money in the environmental fund. That plant is an environmental shell:
air through the floor, etc. So I can't see a lot of
problems unless just pure boredom sets in among the
people and they find ways to create some diversions.
They don't even want to rotate jobs in there. Of all
places, you would think that would require more job
rotation. An engine plant is quite interesting by
contrast; people move around from the machining end
to the assembly end, there's a lot of room for movement through that plant, for experience with new
carburetion devices, with all sorts of new adaptions
to machining changes. That's an ongoing process.
But in that [SKF] plant, a guy can work 30 years
right in the same job and never see a change in the
process unless they use higher speed tooling or
better metallurgy. And that puts a different light
on it. So management says, "Almost anybody can be
manager here, so we'll agree with the union and give
them what they want." But you can't appoint the
plant manager obviously. It's just the line foreman
you appoint, who is nothing more than a group leader
at that point. That type of work in a plant presents
a whole different set of problems and responses to
problems.

BIRGER VIKLUND (SWEDISH CENTER FOR WORKING LIFE):
No national agreement on co-determination has been
reached in the private sector yet, but in the public
sector it is done quite a lot and we have both national
and local agreements. We're publishing next week a
study on the city of Eksiltuna where 82% of those
interviewed there said yes, they had much more say

today than they had before the [Employee Participation] Act. Twenty-five percent said they had "enough influence" – I wonder how much influence they want to have.

One interesting aspect of the Act is to what extent unions and workers should participate in management and sit in joint committees and design operations and where and when should they negotiate these matters at the bargaining table. This is a problem that will be dealt with very much in the future, also in the agreements to come in the private sector. Shall we go to joint committees? Or shall we negotiate the American way?

The answer is different at different levels and it depends on the kind of operation. One result of our research is the finding that the traditional union attitude is to sit in joint committees when the union has not got a program of its own – that is the tradition now – and negotiate when the union knows what it wants. Why not do it the other way around?

When you sit in joint committees when the union doesn't have a real program, then you become co-opted. But if you do it the other way around, you will sit in joint committees only _after_ the union has established its own program and really knows what it wants. _Then_ they can sit in joint committees. But until then, negotiate.

FINAL COMMENT

Despite the eight-hour day, the forty-hour week, the paid holidays and paid vacations that would strike our grandparents as too good to be true, work continues to be the central part of most days for most of our lives. Not only do we spend most of our creative energy on the job, our jobs also determine the quality of our leisure time, whether we have energy left for kids and conversation or whether we settle on the sofa to doze in front of the TV. We all know that something is missing on the job, that things could be different and better. But we spend little time thinking about what it is or what we could do about it. After all, there's a job to be done.

As the roundtable discussion that concluded the workshop suggests, as a group we drew no conclusions. Had we tried, the task would not have been easy. American and Scandinavian realities are far too complex and far too different to say simply: "This should be transferred to the U.S." or "That ought to be rejected out of hand." Had the group drafted a final statement, the bottom line unquestionably would have been that while the Scandinavian accomplishments in restructuring industrial relations are impressive (though certainly not without fault), they offer no panacea for the United States. Our solutions, like those of others, must fit our conditions.

But we can profit from the experience of others, both from their successes and their mistakes.

In the latter half of the last century, journeymen continued the old guild custom of traveling across national boundaries to work in their crafts. Their journeys not only spread knowledge of new processes of production and skills but they also spread the ideas of trade unionism. You worked alongside others in

your trade in other towns in other countries for severa
years while you traveled, and you knew foreign journeymen in your shop or union local back home. Personal
acquaintance with foreign conditions and foreign co-
workers produced a cross-fertilization of ideas about
how work was and how it ought to be.

The world of the itinerant journeyman came to an
end with the imposition of passport, visa, and work
permit requirements during World War I and its after-
math. But we can replicate some of that cross-fertilization of ideas in the modern setting. One comes,
sees, hears, understands, and takes something useful
home: the sense that things could be otherwise. That
can only be disquieting. As Bob Buffenbarger put it
in his report to his union, the International Association of Machinists, "How dare you...take a run of the
mill union member who has achieved [his] goals of a
family to be proud of, a home, a skill and interesting
job, a good voting record and self-satisfaction --
take such a person and in two weeks rattle that compla-
cency to the bone?"

In working life and industrial relations, as in so
many other areas, we see our own reality most clearly
when we look at that of others.